Born to Shine: Unlocking Happiness

Caleb Lounds

Independently published

Copyright © 2023 Caleb Lounds

ISBN-13: 979-8386627645 (Paperback)
ISBN-13: 979-8386628000 (Hardcover)

Contents

Introduction

Positive thinking is an essential part of living a fulfilling and successful life. It allows us to focus on the good things in our lives, rather than the bad. It helps us to recognize and appreciate our strengths and talents, rather than dwelling on our weaknesses and failures. Positive thinking can also help us to become more resilient in the face of adversity, as it helps us to focus on the solutions to our problems rather than the problems themselves.

However, it is important to remember that positive thinking does not come naturally to everyone. It takes practice and dedication to learn how to think positively. We must make a conscious effort to challenge our negative thoughts and to focus on the good in our lives. We must also be mindful of how our environment can influence our thinking and adjust our surroundings accordingly.

With practice and dedication, positive thinking can become second nature. We can learn to recognize the positives in our lives, to appreciate our strengths and talents, and to remain resilient even in the face of adversity. We can learn to focus on solutions rather than problems, and to create a brighter future for ourselves and those around us.

Chapter 1: Introduction to Positive Thinking: Understanding Its Benefits

Are you ready to learn about the incredible benefits of positive thinking? Positive thinking is a powerful tool that can positively improve the quality of our lives. It can help us to become more successful, healthy, and content in our day-to-day lives. In order to reap the benefits of positive thinking, it is important to understand what this concept really is and how to practice it. This chapter will provide an overview of positive thinking and discuss the numerous benefits associated with it.

What is Positive Thinking?

Positive thinking is a type of mental attitude and behavior focused on possibility and optimism rather than fear and pessimism. People who engage in positive thinking focus on solutions rather than problems and look for successes instead of failure. They strive to identify ways to make the most of their circumstances instead of dwelling on what might inhibit them.

Positive thinking can also be defined as a mental state of mind focused on allowing love, success, and happiness to manifest in one's life. The practice of positive thinking can bring an individual into alignment with their higher self, allowing them to achieve a greater sense of clarity, purpose, and overall well-being.

Positive thinking is a powerful tool for creating a happier, more fulfilling life. It's about looking at the bright side of life and having faith that things will work out. It's about believing in yourself and having hope for the future. It's about being grateful for what you have and having an optimistic outlook on life.

But what are the benefits of positive thinking?

Benefits of Positive Thinking

The many benefits of positive thinking have been studied and explored over the years. Some of the more notable benefits of positive thinking include:

• Improved Mental Health:

Positive thinking can result in improved mental wellbeing, increased clarity, and an overall sense of peace.

Positive thinking can help you be more content with life and find joy in the present moment. It can help you be more mindful of your thoughts and to appreciate the good in life.

• Improved Physical Health:

Positive thinking also has many physical health benefits. These include improved immune system functioning, lower blood pressure, and increased longevity.

Positive thinking has been linked to improved physical and mental health. It can help reduce stress and anxiety and make you feel more relaxed.

• Increased Resilience:

Those who practice positive thinking build up a degree of inner strength and resilience which can help them to cope with difficult situations and life challenges.

• Improved Relationships:

Positive thinking can help you create deeper and more meaningful relationships with those around you. It can help you be more understanding and compassionate, and to see the best in others.

People who practice positive thinking are more likely to be confident and engaged in social interactions, leading to stronger and healthier relationships.

• Increased Productivity:

Positive thinking can also lead to increased productivity, as individuals are better able to focus and stay on task when their minds are focused on the positive possibilities instead of the potential negative outcomes.

Positive thinking can help you be more successful in your career. It can help you stay motivated and inspired, and to take positive action towards your goals.

The benefits of positive thinking are numerous. It can help in all areas of life and can create lasting changes. Understanding the power of positive thinking is the first step to creating a happier, more fulfilling life.

Conclusion

Positive thinking is a powerful tool for success, health, and happiness. This chapter provided an introduction to positive thinking, including a definition of what it is, and the many benefits associated with it. With this knowledge, you are now prepared to dive deeper into the practice of positive thinking and to begin reaping the many benefits it has to offer.

Chapter 2:
Becoming Aware of Negative Thoughts

It is important to understand that negative thoughts are a normal part of life and will occur no matter how hard we try to avoid them. The key to managing your negative thoughts lies in becoming aware of their presence. Once we become aware of these negative thoughts, we can begin to make changes to our thinking patterns and reactions so that we can move forward positively.

When we become aware of our thoughts, we can start to identify the source of our negativity. For example, are you noticing negative thoughts about yourself because you compare yourself to what you see on social media? Or does your work environment cause you to think critically of yourself? It's important to understand where the negative thoughts are coming from so we can address them more effectively.

Likewise projecting referred negative thoughts onto others is another unhealthy behavior that involves taking one's own negative thoughts and feelings and projecting them onto others. This type of behavior often occurs when an individual is having difficulty accepting their own negative emotions, so they displace those emotions onto someone else. This can be a very destructive behavior, as it can damage relationships and lead to negative outcomes for everyone involved. It is important to learn healthy coping strategies that focus on understanding and accepting one's own negative thoughts and feelings instead of projecting them onto others.

Negative thoughts can be a powerful force, especially when they are projected onto others due to past traumas. When someone has faced difficult experiences in the past, they may find themselves unable to let go of their pain and instead project their negative thoughts onto those around them. This can manifest in a variety of ways, such as over-critical behavior, blaming others for one's own problems, being overly suspicious and distrusting of others or an overall negative attitude. It can be difficult for those who are on the receiving end of this negative energy, as it can make them feel like they can't live up to your expectations or as though they are always doing something wrong and may make it hard for them to feel seen or understood. Fortunately, there are methods of healing from past traumas and learning to be more aware of one's thoughts and feelings. Through self-reflection, mindfulness, and in some cases therapy, it is possible to work through negative emotions in a healthy way and learn to be more compassionate with oneself and with others.

Recent studies have shown that the offspring of rats who have been exposed to trauma can inherit a predisposition for negative thinking. The study found that when the babies of rats that were exposed to a stressful situation were exposed to that same situation, they had a heightened level of stress compared to those whose parents had not been exposed to the trauma.

This suggests that the trauma experienced by the parent rat had an impact on the offspring and that they had inherited some of the negative thinking patterns of their parent. This has implications for how we think about the effects of trauma on generations to come. It indicates that we should be mindful of how our own experiences and beliefs can affect our children and grandchildren.

The study also showed that the rats had difficulty shaking off those negative thoughts. Even when the stressful situation had ended, the rats still had a higher level of stress than they did before the experiment began. This suggests that they had difficulty returning to a state of calm and that their minds had become conditioned to respond to a stressful situation in a negative way.

These findings suggest that animals, including humans, may be genetically predisposed to negative thinking. This has implications for how we approach our own mental health, as well as how we interact with others. It is important to be aware of this predisposition and to take steps to reduce or eliminate it. This could mean taking the time to challenge negative thoughts, engaging in positive activities, or if necessary, seeking professional help.

It is also important to be aware of the impact of trauma on our own lives. We should take the time to challenge our own negative thoughts and to focus on what we can control. We should also be mindful of how our own experiences may affect our children and grandchildren. By doing this, we can help break the cycle of negative thinking and create a brighter future for the generations to come.

Once you become aware of the source of the negative thoughts, you can start to explore ways of changing your reaction to them. This may include challenging your thinking patterns by asking yourself questions like, "Is this really true?" or "How might I reframe this thought into something more positive?" Additionally, you can try to focus on the present moment and be mindful of what you're feeling or thinking in order to stop the negative thought from spiraling.

Being aware of your negative thoughts is the first step to breaking their cycle. When we become conscious of our thinking, we can start to take steps to make positive changes. This can have a drastically positive effect on our mental well-being, leading to increased feelings of contentment and self-compassion.

Chapter 3:
Becoming Aware of Projected Thoughts

One of the most important steps in stopping the habit of projecting negative thoughts onto others is to become aware of the fact that we are doing it in the first place. First, take some time to reflect on situations in which you might have been quick to judge someone for their behavior, opinion, or anything else. Notice the emotions underlying the thoughts you were having, as these scenarios can reveal what kind of negative thoughts you may be subconsciously projecting onto others.

Once you can recognize when you are projecting negative thoughts, you can begin to practice self-awareness when it comes to your emotions. Pay attention to the feelings that come up in different situations and practice cultivating an internal dialogue that acknowledges your feelings and allows them to be expressed without judgement.

Susan Realizes She is Projecting Negative Thoughts

Susan had always been an optimist. She had seen the world as full of possibility and had always strove to make the best of every situation. But lately, she had begun to notice a shift in her thinking. She found herself getting frustrated more easily and projecting negative thoughts onto those around her. This led her to feel distrusting of the people she felt like she should be close to.

At first, she tried to ignore it. But the more she tried to push it away, the more persistent it became. Until one day, she finally realized what was going on. She was projecting her own negative thoughts and feelings onto others, due to the trauma she had experienced in her past.

Once she had this realization, she was able to recognize the patterns in her behavior and to start making changes. She began to challenge her negative thoughts and to focus on the positives. She started to appreciate the strengths and talents of those around her and to be more mindful of the environment she was in.

Susan knew that in order to create lasting change, she had to take a deeper look at her past. She began to explore the trauma she had experienced in her childhood and to understand how it had impacted her life. She started to recognize her own patterns of behavior and to take responsibility for her own thoughts and choices.

She also began to practice self-care, taking time each day to focus on her own wellbeing. She started to practice mindfulness, allowing herself to be present in the moment and to acknowledge her feelings without judgement. She also began to reach out for support from her friends and family, allowing them to be a source of comfort and understanding.

Through this process of self-reflection and self-care, Slowly, Susan was finally able to move forward. She was able to make peace with her past and to create a brighter future for herself. She had finally found a way to break the cycle of negative thinking and to live a life of joy and peace.

Chapter 4:
Exercising Self-Compassion

Once you can become aware of your negative thoughts and if, when and how you may be projecting negative thoughts onto others, you can begin to practice self-compassion. Treat yourself with the same kindness and understanding you would extend to a friend or family member and challenge the negative self-talk that often arises. Offer yourself words of encouragement and notice if your perspective on the situation changes when you practice being compassionate towards yourself.

At the same time, remember that mistakes are inevitable and part of being human. Use moments of negative thinking and negative

projection as learning experiences and to drive
you to be more conscious of your thoughts in
the future.

Joe Learns to Exercises Self-Compassion

Joe had always been a perfectionist. He had
grown up believing that he needed to be
perfect in order to be accepted, and that any
mistakes he made were unforgivable. He was
hard on himself and had difficulty being gentle
and understanding with himself.

But one day, Joe had a realization. He
realized that he was not perfect, and that it
was ok to make mistakes. He began to practice
self-compassion. He started to recognize his
own strengths and to forgive himself for his
mistakes. He allowed himself to be imperfect,
and to make mistakes without judgement.

Joe started to practice mindfulness,
reminding himself to be present in the
moment and to acknowledge his feelings
without judgement. He also began to reach out
for support from his friends and family,

allowing them to be a source of comfort and understanding. He started to take time for himself each day, focusing on his own wellbeing and finding joy in simple moments.

Through this process, Joe was finally able to make peace with himself. He was able to recognize his own potential and to create a brighter future for himself. He had finally found a way to practice self-compassion and to live a life filled with joy and peace.

Chapter 5:
Cultivating Empathy

Positive thinking is a powerful tool for creating a happier, more fulfilling life. But this kind of thinking doesn't just happen overnight – rather, it requires consistent effort and practice. One of the keys to developing positive thinking is cultivating empathy.

When we practice cultivating empathy towards those around us, it can make it easier to avoid our negative thoughts as well as projecting our own negative thoughts. Instead of quickly jumping to judgement, take a step back and observe the situation with a curious and compassionate eye. Challenge yourself to explore the feelings of others before making any immediate assumptions and try to put yourself in their shoes.

This practice will not only help reduce negative thinking and the projecting of negative thoughts onto others, but also create a sense of connection that can lead to greater fulfillment.

Empathy is the ability to understand and share the feelings of another. It allows us to better understand the perspectives and experiences of others, which can help us develop more positive thinking. Here are some tips to help you cultivate empathy and develop a more positive mindset:

1. Listen actively. Listening is a critical aspect of empathy. When someone is talking to you, try to focus on what they're saying rather than plotting out what you want to say in response. Listening with an open, understanding ear can help you gain insight into how someone else is feeling, which can help you develop more positive thinking.

2. Put yourself in their shoes. When trying to understand someone else's feelings, try to imagine what it would be like to be in their situation. This will help you better understand

their perspective and develop more empathy, which can lead to more positive thinking.

3. Show your support. Showing support is a powerful way to demonstrate your empathy. Letting someone know that you're there for them and that you care can help them feel supported and understood, which can help them develop more positive thinking.

4. Practice gratitude. Practicing gratitude is a great way to cultivate empathy. By counting your blessings, you can develop a greater appreciation for the good things in life and be more aware of the experiences of others.

Empathy is an important skill for developing positive thinking. It can help us better understand how others are feeling and create more meaningful relationships with those around us. By following the tips above, you can become a more empathetic person and develop a more positive mindset.

Chapter 6:
Practicing Mindfulness

Mindfulness is a practice of being present in the moment and focusing on the sensations, thoughts, and feelings that come up in any given situation. When you take the time to be mindful, your attention may naturally be drawn away from any negative thoughts that may be sneaking into your mind.

Practicing mindfulness can be as simple as taking a few minutes each day to sit in stillness and observe your thoughts without judgement. You can also practice being mindful in everyday activities, such as doing the dishes or taking a walk in nature.

By using techniques like these to practice mindfulness, you can learn to stay conscious of your thoughts and avoid projecting them onto others.

Chapter 7:
Recognizing and Challenging Negative Beliefs

Once you have identified some of the underlying beliefs, the next step is to recognize and challenge those beliefs. When it comes to challenging negative beliefs, it is important to have a good understanding of the facts. Relying on rational thinking and focusing on facts instead of feelings can help challenge and replace many of the irrational beliefs and assumptions.

One way to do this is to question the accuracy of the belief. This can be done by gathering evidence that challenges the belief.

This can be done through research, observation, and/or personal experience. For example, if a person believes that they save reject them, they can challenge this belief by remembering past relationships in which they felt accepted and valued.

Another strategy is to reframe the belief. This involves restructuring the belief in order to make it more realistic and helpful. This can be done by looking for examples that contradict the belief or coming up with alternatives that are more balanced. For example, if someone believes that they are always going to fail, they can try to reframe this belief into one that is more positive, such as "I am capable of succeeding if I work hard and don't give up."

Finally, it is important to learn how to manage the negative thoughts and feelings associated with the belief. This can include using distraction and relaxation techniques, or engaging in positive activities that help to boost self-esteem.

By recognizing and challenging negative beliefs, you can start to gain confidence and control of your life. With practice and guidance, this process can be empowering and lead to improved mental health.

Chapter 8:
Developing an Unshakable Belief in Yourself

One of the most important parts of developing an unshakable belief in yourself is learning to trust your instincts and intuition. In order to do this, it is important to look inward and to become aware of your own strengths and weaknesses. It is important to know what you are capable of, and also to recognize when you need help or guidance. Knowing your limits and abilities will help you to set realistic expectations and goals and to move forward in life.

Another important part of believing in yourself is to focus on positive thinking. This includes learning to recognize and celebrate your successes as well as learning to acknowledge and accept mistakes. It can be difficult to stay positive, but it is important to remember to let go of negative thoughts and feelings that might be lingering.

The third tip for developing an unshakable belief in yourself is to take action. Believe in yourself enough to take action and put in the work that is necessary to reach your goals. Taking action will give you a sense of accomplishment and will show yourself that you are capable of achieving what you set out to do.

Finally, practice self-care. Take the time to rest, exercise, and to do things that make you feel good about yourself. This could be anything from getting a massage or a facial to taking an extra hour for yourself each day. Taking time for yourself is one of the best ways to build an unshakable belief in yourself and to stay mindful of your own mental and physical well-being.

Chapter 9:
Cultivating a Positive Mental Climate

When it comes to creating a positive mental climate for yourself, it is important to recognize the power of your thoughts and identify techniques that can help you stay in a positive mindset.

Focusing On The Positive

The power of positivity is an extremely important factor when it comes to cultivating a positive mental climate. When you find yourself focusing on the negative aspects in your life, take some time to think about the good things instead. Make a conscious effort to be optimistic, as optimism helps us stay motivated and find solutions to problems. Make sure to focus on the things you can change, rather than dwelling on the things you can't.

Meditation

Meditation can help to bring clarity to your thoughts and calm your mind. This can help you to stay in a more positive frame of mind and can be a great tool for reducing stress. There are many different types of meditation to choose from, take some time to explore and find one that works for you.

Communication

The establishment of healthy communication is another important aspect of cultivating a positive mental climate. Whether it is talking to a friend, a family member or a colleague, finding people to talk to can help us to verbalize our feelings and focus on solutions rather than dwelling on the issues. It's also important to take time to listen. By hearing what other people have to say, and sharing your own thoughts and experiences, you can gain new insights and perspective.

Self-Care

Taking care of yourself is a necessary and integral part of staying positive. Make sure to prioritize rest, eating well, exercising, and engaging in activities that bring you joy. Taking time to relax and enjoy yourself can help to give you the energy and motivation to keep a positive outlook.

Setting Goals

Creating objectives that you can meet can be one of the most powerful tools in cultivating a positive mental climate. Having a roadmap for how you want to achieve your goals can be extremely helpful, as it will give you a sense of focus and direction. As you complete tasks and goals, you'll be more likely to stay in a positive state of mind and be more motivated to continue striving for your objectives.

Finally, be kind and gentle with yourself. Accepting that life is not perfect, that we all have struggles, and that there's no such thing as a "perfect" path will help you to remain positive and develop resilience in facing life's challenges.

Chapter 10:
Reinforcing Your Positive Thinking

In order to build a solid foundation of positive thinking habits, it is important to reinforce your positive thinking. This means that you consciously and intentionally remind yourself of the positive thoughts and beliefs you have chosen to focus on. Here are a few ways you can reinforce your positive thinking:

1. Make a Daily Affirmation: A daily affirmation is a positive statement you make each day that helps focus your mind and energy on the positive. Writing a daily affirmation on a card or in a notebook and using it as a reminder can be very helpful.

2. Regularly Spend Time with Positive People: Positive people help to reinforce your positive thinking and help keep you from engaging in negative thought patterns. Find an uplifting group to hang out with that shares your values and attitudes about life.

3. Take Time for Reflection and Meditation: Practicing meditation and reflection can help you stay present and focused on the positive aspects of your life. Spending a few moments each day reflecting on the good in your life can greatly improve your long-term attitude and outlook.

4. Take Time for Free Activity: Taking time for free activity such as walks, hobbies, or simply lounging can help to refuel you energy and provide opportunities for positive thinking. Set aside regular times in your day to do something that you enjoy without any other agenda.

5. Receive Positive Feedback: When you make an effort to be positive, it is also important to receive positive feedback from others. Make a point of asking friends and family to tell you a positive thought they have about you periodically. Make sure to thank

them for their input when they do. This not only reinforces their positive feedback; it also reinforces your positive thinking.

By reinforcing your positive thinking, you can build a solid foundation for healthier, more positive habits and beliefs. A few small changes each day can help create lasting changes in your life. Positive thinking leads to greater happiness, better relationships, and improved overall health and well being.

Chapter 11:
Visualizing Your Goals and Dreams

Visualizing your goals and dreams can be a powerful tool to help you stay focused, motivated and on the right path to achieving them. Visualization is the practice of picturing in your mind's eye the desired outcome or goal. It is the act of seeing yourself already having achieved what it is you want. Visualization can be used as a means of both motivation and achieving clarity regarding your goals and dreams.

Firstly, you need to clearly envision what it is you desire to achieve. Get clear and specific in your mind, think of anything that would help you visualize your dreams and goals. Do you want to be healthier? Picture yourself with a perfect physique, eating healthy foods and exercising regularly. Do you want to be financially successful? Think about what it would look like to have all things that come with financial success, a nice house, expensive car, etc.

Once you've visualized your desired outcome, use it as a motivating tool. Keep it in the forefront of your mind, constantly reminding yourself why you are working toward the goal you have set. This will give you the drive and motivation to keep on pushing towards the achievement of those dreams and goals.

The next step is to make a plan. Write down what steps need to be taken to get you closer to achieving your dreams and goals. Use visualization to help guide your plans. Break them down into small, attainable goals that you can work towards. For example, if you plan on writing a book, envision each chapter, the title, and all of the other details that go into it.

Finally, make it a habit to revisit your goals and dreams with visualization. Dedicate a few moments each day to imaging how life would be once your goals and dreams have been achieved. Have faith in the process and keep believing that your dreams and goals can one day become a reality. Visualization works, but you have to put in the time and dedication that is required to make it happen. With enough determination and drive, you can turn your goals and dreams into reality.

Visualizing Success: Isabella's Story

Isabella was an ambitious girl with big dreams, but she was also very shy and lacked self-confidence. People often told her she was too small and too timid to accomplish her goals. But Isabella was determined to prove them wrong. She began to practice visualization and positive affirmations to boost her self-confidence and focus on her goals. She imagined winning the school essay contest, getting accepted into her dream college, and achieving all of her goals.

Isabella decided to take small steps towards her dreams. She worked hard at school, writing essays and studying for exams, and wrote the best essay she could for the contest. She also applied to her dream college, not letting her doubts and fears get in the way.

And then, one day, she received the news that she had been accepted. She was ecstatic, and it was just the beginning. Isabella continued to work hard and put in the effort, and eventually achieved all of her goals.

Through her determination and visualization, Isabella proved all of her doubters wrong. She showed that with hard work and a positive attitude, anything is possible. She also learned the importance of believing in herself and never giving up on her dreams.

Chapter 12:
Embracing Gratitude and Generosity

In life, it is important to maintain a sense of gratitude and generosity. These two acts allow us to both appreciate the blessings in our lives and contribute to the greater good. Through embracing gratitude and generosity, people can lead a life that is happier and more meaningful.

Gratitude is an important life lesson to learn, and recognizing the things we are thankful for can make all the difference. Expressing gratitude on a daily basis can bring a sense of contentment and fulfillment. There may be difficult days, but the knowledge that we do have things to be thankful for can help us get through them.

Generosity is also an important part of life. It can be expressed in different ways, whether it's through donating time or money, volunteering in the community, or simply helping out a neighbor. Generosity is also a great way to meet others, build relationships, and spread kindness and goodwill.

Living with an attitude of gratitude and generosity can have a profound effect on our lives. It can bring us joy, peace, and a sense of satisfaction in our lives. When we practice gratitude and generosity it can help us appreciate all that we have and can also benefit those around us.

So, take a moment each day to think about the good in your life and be generous to those around you. Embrace a life of gratitude and generosity and allow it to enrich your life.

Chapter 13:
Shifting Your Perspective for More Positivity

Once you become aware that cognition, or thought patterns, are influencing the way you think and feel, it's easier to recognize the thoughts that may be getting in the way of more positive feelings.

One way to shift your perspective for more positivity is to focus on what's going right and what you can do to make things even better. This requires an intentional reconfiguration of your thoughts and can help you move away from negative emotions.

Start by tuning into your thought patterns and recognizing the thoughts that lead to feeling down, such as "I can't do anything right." Once you become aware of those thoughts, consciously reframe them in more positive terms. For example, try replacing them with "I can do this" or "I am capable of achieving my goals."

You can also try reframing situations to focus on what you can control. Try to recognize areas that are in your power to change and make the most of those opportunities. This means capitalizing on your resources, such as your support network or the tools you're able to access. It also means being mindful of situations that you can't control, such as a global pandemic or a particularly difficult work situation.

Not all perspective shifts will be easy. Habitual thoughts can be difficult to break, but it's worth the effort to become aware of them and do the work to shift your thinking. Invest in yourself with activities that make you feel relaxed and fulfilled, such as yoga, journaling, or self-care rituals.

Practice gratitude and focus on things to appreciate in your life. Allow yourself to enjoy small moments and start to focus on focusing on a brighter future.

Negativity may always be a part of life, but by practicing kindness to yourself and building up more positive thoughts, you can move away from it and toward a more positive perspective.

Chapter 14:
Fostering an Attitude of Gratitude

It is important to foster an attitude of gratitude in all members of your family or business. Being grateful for the good times and for all the blessings that come our way can help us stay connected and help maintain peace and harmony.

One way to foster an attitude of gratitude is to set aside a moment each day to reflect and be thankful for what we have. This could be a moment of prayer, a few moments of silent reflection, or a simple recognition of the good things that have happened that day.

Encourage your children to express gratitude and to be grateful for all the good things life has to offer. Make it a fun and enjoyable experience where everyone can contribute. Start a gratitude jar and encourage everyone to add one thing per day that they are thankful for.

Recognize the positive contributions of others to your life and family and show your appreciation. Let others know that you appreciate and recognize their hard work, dedication, and good intentions.

As a family or business, take time to recognize accomplishments, special moments and giving. Being grateful can bring people closer and help cultivate a positive environment.

Finally, recognize and appreciate the natural world - the sunrises and sunsets, the birds chirping and the flowers blooming. Gratitude for the beauty of nature can help keep us grounded and provide a feeling of contentment and joy.

Chapter 15:
Practicing Self- Compassion and Acceptance

Self-compassion and acceptance are two essential aspects of mental health that you should strive for. Practicing self-compassion and acceptance can help foster positive feelings and coping mechanisms and enable you to become more resilient in the face of difficult situations.

The first step to practicing self-compassion and acceptance is to become aware of how you talk to yourself. When you experience negative emotions or self-doubt, take a step back and recognize that the way you're talking to yourself is not comfortable or supportive.

Instead, recognize that you are in the process of learning and growing.

You can start to practice self-compassion by taking time to check in and comfort yourself when you feel stressed or overwhelmed. Reflect on what you have accomplished or do something that brings you joy and satisfaction. Be mindful of when you start to feel uncomfortable or criticize yourself. Take a few moments to practice self-compassion and remember that you are human and capable of making mistakes. Acknowledge your weaknesses but also recognize your strengths and all of your efforts so far. Instead of getting stuck in a cycle of negative thinking and self-criticism, focus on your positive qualities and take steps to make improvements where needed.

You can also practice self-acceptance by honoring yourself and all of your experiences, both positive and negative. Instead of measuring yourself up to someone else's standards, focus on who you are and what you want to become. Self-acceptance is not an instant process; it takes time to be kind to yourself and to recognize that you don't have to meet all of your own expectations 100% of the time.

Lastly, understand that self-compassion and acceptance is a process and something that you will continue to work on over time. With enough practice and dedication, you can take steps towards finding a sense of inner peace and joy.

Chapter 16:
Enhancing Your Self-Worth and Confidence

Self-worth is how you feel about yourself and the value you place on yourself. It is the inner source of security and strength that benefits you in all areas of life. Having strong self-worth gives you the confidence to reach out, take risks, and persevere through life's challenges. It also gives you the courage to face your fears, speak your truth, and follow your dreams. Unfortunately, many people struggle to maintain a healthy sense of self-worth and can experience far-reaching consequences if it's not addressed. Over time, these feelings of helplessness and worthlessness can adversely affect relationships, work, finances, and self-care.

In order to improve your self-worth, it takes practice and dedication. The following are some ideas for enhancing your self-worth and confidence:

1. Work on accepting yourself. One way to improve your self-worth is to focus on accepting yourself for who you are, including any mistakes or challenges you have faced. It's important to remember that we all go through different experiences in life, and that everyone has his or her own challenges to overcome. Accepting yourself allows you to move past your mistakes and take responsibility for your actions instead of allowing them to define who you are.

2. Practice self-care. Taking care of yourself is essential in order to maintain good physical and mental health. Self-care can involve a variety of activities, like getting adequate sleep, exercise, eating well, and engaging in hobbies and activities you enjoy. Additionally, make sure to nurture yourself emotionally by finding ways to relax, practice mindfulness, and build supportive relationships with family and friends.

3. Build your skills. Taking steps to build your skills can help boost your self-confidence and self-worth. Whether it's learning a new language, developing a new skill, or obtaining a certification, taking the time to build your skills shows your commitment to personal growth and achieving your goals.

4. Act authentically. Part of feeling good about yourself is understanding who you are and being true to yourself. Authenticity involves being honest, genuinely expressing your feelings, and avoiding the pressure of performing for the approval of others. When you are true to yourself, you are more likely to access your inner source of strength and confidence.

5. Celebrate accomplishments and successes. Accomplishments and successes provide opportunities to recognize your accomplishments and boost your self-worth. For instance, if you are learning a new skill or accomplishment, take time to appreciate the progress you have made, no matter how small. Additionally, find ways to celebrate your successes by indulging in something you enjoy, like a special treat or taking a break to relax.

By focusing on the tips above, you can enhance your self-worth and confidence, allowing you to step into your power and courageously thrive in life.

Chapter 17:
Cultivating Self-Love and Respect

For many of us, cultivating self-love and respect is a long and difficult process. We often battle negative emotions, self-doubt, and the fear of failure. We struggle to break down the walls of insecurity we have built around us, and to learn to accept and love ourselves.

The best way to cultivate self-love and respect is to start by recognizing your strengths. Take a breath and make a list of all the things that you are proud of. These don't have to be big accomplishments or major life events. You can include small everyday acts of courage, kindness, and self-care. Making this list is a way of giving yourself permission to take the time to appreciate yourself and what you have achieved.

Once you recognize your strengths, it is important to surround yourself with people who recognize and appreciate your worth. Don't be afraid to open up to people you trust and talk about your feelings, dreams and accomplishments. It does not matter if these people are family, mentors, or friends. Being heard and supported can motivate and encourage you to keep going even when you feel down.

Self-care is also important to cultivating self-love and respect. When you take the time to nurture yourself, you will better be able to recognize and appreciate your worth. Make it a priority to do something that you enjoy every day. This could include reading, writing, listening to music, cooking, pursuing a hobby, exercising, or playing a sport. Whatever makes you feel good, make the time to do it.

Lastly, spend some time in gratitude. Gratitude is a great way to keep track of the positive things in your life and appreciate them. When you focus on the positive, it can motivate you to continue to grow in self-love and respect.

Although cultivating self-love and respect is a difficult process, if you persevere and commit to doing it, you will eventually reach a place of self-love, respect, and contentment.

Chapter 18:
The Power of Affirmations

In Chapter 18, we explore the power of affirmations. Affirmations are a powerful tool for achieving success, unlocking potential, and amplifying mental and emotional strength.

Simply put, affirmations are positive statements that you say or think about yourself or about a goal or area of focus in your life. Affirmations can be used to instill confidence, boost motivation, and create a lasting change in your life.

The power of affirmative statements can be traced back to the days of affirmations and mantras. Mantras were originally used by ancient sages to help focus their concentration on one goal and develop specific powers.

These days, affirmations are often used to motivate, inspire, and create the positive change we want to see in our lives. They can help us to be more self-confident, optimistic, and successful in all areas of life.

When used correctly, affirmations can help you focus your energy on attaining the desired outcome. Repeating the same affirmation several times can help them to take root in your mind and stay there, with the positive effect increasing as you say the affirmations more and more.

Affirmations can be used to counter negative thoughts and communication which may otherwise have been difficult to ignore. Affirmations are particularly powerful when used at times when you're feeling down or defeated or are in need of extra motivation and encouragement.

As Affirmations continue to become more and more popular, it's essential that you use the power of affirmations in the most effective way. To ensure that your affirmations are successful, make sure that the statement you are using is true, attainable, and realistic.

The best way to use Affirmations is to pair them with Visualizations. When you're visualizing and saying the affirmations together, you're initiating an important process at the subconscious level.

When paired correctly with Visualizations and emotion, affirmations can be incredibly powerful at releasing the belief patterns and habits that have been keeping you from achieving the goals that you have set for yourself.

Affirmations can be used in many areas of life and can help with anything from gaining self-confidence to achieving your career goals and discovering more success in the process. By repetition of positive affirmations, we can instill these principles in our minds, making them part of our lives and reaping the rewards of their power.

Chapter 19:
Practicing Mindfulness Continued

As we discussed earlier in this book mindfulness is the practice of being conscious and aware of what is happening in the present moment. It involves paying attention to the present without forming judgments or striving for something else. Mindfulness has become a popular way to manage stress, anxiety, and depression, as well as enhance physical and mental health.

Mindfulness is not a one-size-fits-all practice. There are different approaches and techniques, and it is up to the individual to decide which works best for them. It is important to find activities that can help bring the individual back to the present instead of being overwhelmed by anxieties or worries.

The first step in practicing mindfulness is to pay attention to what is happening in the present moment. To start, one can focus on their breathing. This is a great way to start as it is often the first thing we notice when we become mindful. By focusing on your breathing, it can help ground you in the present moment and help bring your thoughts and feelings into awareness.

Another great way to practice mindfulness is to use a guided meditation. This can consist of listening to a soothing voice, focusing on visualizations, or using affirmations. This approach can be especially helpful for those with a busy mind.

Another popular method for practicing mindfulness is to participate in mindful movement. This can include activities such as yoga, tai chi, and walking meditation. These activities involve movement and focus, which can help one become more aware of their bodies and emotions.

The most important thing to remember when practicing mindfulness is that it is a process. It must be approached with patience and kindness, as it can bring up difficult emotions. By recognizing and accepting these feelings, and not judging them, one can gain greater control over their thoughts and feelings. Over time, with practice, mindfulness can lead to greater wellness and a sense of calm and peace.

Chapter 20:
Avoiding Comparison and Perfectionism

It can be hard to escape comparison and perfectionism in our lives. After all, we live in a world that constantly presents us with expectations of perfection. Whether it be through comparison with others or the idea of achieving the 'perfect life', it can be difficult to feel likc we are ever achieving true success.

However, comparison and perfectionism can be damaging to our self-confidence and emotional well-being. Comparing oneself to others can lead to feelings of jealousy, stress, and low self-esteem. Furthermore, striving for perfection can prevent us from enjoying the process of continued self-improvement and growth.

In order to avoid comparison and perfectionism, it is important to first understand what motivates perfectionism. For example, do you feel like you need to be perfect in order to feel validated? Or are you so focused on reaching a certain goal that you fail to see its beauty? Taking the time to identify why comparison and perfectionism are tempting can help to give us a sense of control over them.

The next step to avoiding comparison and perfectionism is to create a more realistic view of success. This might mean re-defining what success looks like and setting achievable goals. Focus on a balanced lifestyle, knowing that progress and accomplishment come with time and effort. Celebrate the small successes and enjoy the journey of achieving your dreams.

Finally, try to cultivate a sense of gratitude. Instead of focusing on what you don't have or what you "should have", practice counting your blessings. This can help to set your mind at ease and to motivate you to keep striving forward. Don't place too much emphasis on outcomes, as that can be a source of stress. Enjoy the process, celebrate each step of your journey, and be proud of your accomplishments. Above all, remember that you do not need to compare yourself or achieve perfection in order to feel successful.

Chapter 21:
Seeing Challenges as Opportunities

Seeing challenges as opportunities means recognizing that obstacles provide us with chances to learn, develop, and grow. By viewing a challenge as an opportunity, you can make it a source of strength and leverage it to propel yourself forward. This approach empowers you to find solutions instead of dwelling on the setback. Seeing a challenge as an opportunity to increase your knowledge and refine your skills helps you become more self-reliant and confident in your abilities. It also encourages you to think innovatively in the face of roadblocks. Seeing challenges as opportunities ultimately helps you develop the resilience and perseverance necessary to achieve long-term success.

Example 1: Anna's interview

Anna held her breath as the interviewer handed her an unanticipated writing sample. She had been expecting to answer traditional interview questions, not to put her writing abilities to the test. Taking the challenge in stride, she looked it over and smiled. In a way, she was relieved. Being able to put her skills to the test allowed her to showcase her abilities and reflect her personality in the writing. Rather than getting flustered and worried, she took a deep breath and embraced the challenge.

Under the watchful eye of the interviewer, Anna set about highlighting her strengths and displaying her creativity. She looked for ways to use her storytelling abilities to illustrate her points and used clear and concise language to get her ideas across. In a way, the unexpected writing sample became an opportunity to showcase the value she could bring to the team.

When the writing sample was finished, Anna released the breath she had been holding and happily handed the piece back. The interviewer seemed impressed by her efforts and thanked her for her creativity. As Anna prepared to leave and told the interviewer goodbye, she left with the confidence that she had handled the unexpected challenge.

Anna's experience taught her an important lesson: rather than shying away from challenges, she should look for ways to use them as opportunities. By viewing challenges as opportunities, she was able to take control of the situation, turn a hurdle into a steppingstone, and come out on top.

Example 2: Maxine's adventure

After Maxine's adventure in the desert, she was ready to face the world again. As Maxine considered her future, she knew she wanted to stay on the path of self-improvement and personal development. She felt like she had learned so much through the experience, and she wanted to make sure she implemented the lessons into her everyday life.

Maxine decided to use the lessons learned in the desert to her advantage. She thought about how she could take risks without feeling like she was always in control, and what it would be like to make mistakes without fearing failure or judgement.

In order to put her new skills to work, Maxine started looking for challenges in her life and found plenty of them. Instead of shying away from them, Maxine decided to take a new approach. She considered them as opportunities for growth and for testing her newly acquired skills.

Rather than letting fear hold her back, Maxine began to see the challenges she faced as gifts. She linked them to her personal growth and development, and as a result, she was able to stay focused on the good, rather than being overcome by the bad.

Maxine was amazed at how much she was able to achieve through being open to challenges. Every time she conquered one, she felt a renewed sense of strength and resilience that she hadn't experienced before. With this newfound confidence and courage, she was able to tap into her creative potential and start embracing more challenges and opportunities in her life.

Maxine had started to change her perspective on life, and it made a big difference in terms of how she saw the world. She was empowered to take on any challenges that came her way with confidence, and over time she was able to build a strong foundation for success.

Maxine smiled as she looked back on her journey, and she was grateful for how far she had come. She now knew that if she continued to take risks and embrace challenges with courage, then she would be able to achieve any goal she set her mind to. She was determined to keep growing as a person and making a positive impact on the world. Her time in the desert had certainly paid off.

Chapter 22:
Seeking Out Growth

Seeking out growth opportunities means actively looking for ways to advance one's career, develop new skills, and increase their job prospects or earning potential. It involves taking initiative to identify new opportunities or create them oneself. This could include furthering your education or certifications, networking with industry leaders, or finding new markets to break into.

Example 1: John's Journey to Unlock His Potential

John is always on the lookout for opportunities to grow and develop his skills. He recently enrolled in an online course to learn a new software package and is excited to learn more. He's committed to networking with experienced professionals in his field to create a stronger network. Additionally, John is actively seeking out opportunities to attend seminars, conferences, or other events related to his industry. He believes that by exposing himself to these activities, he will gain valuable knowledge about the industry, connect with like-minded professionals, and learn the latest trends. But John also knows that by maintaining his positive thinking and putting himself out there, he will draw his goals to him. He is confident that these experiences will provide him with the opportunity to gain valuable insights, insight that will ultimately help him unlock his potential and advance his career.

Example 2: Professional Growth for Jane.

The past few months have been filled with personal and professional growth for Jane. She has continually pushed herself and reached out to cross-disciplinary professionals to explore new opportunities. But now, Jane was feeling the need to go just a bit further, to seek out growth opportunities to take her career to the next level.

So, she did what any ambitious professional would do. She asked for help.

Jane reached out to her network, made an effort to attend local events and utilize available resources, and even took advantage of available online services. No matter how much effort she put into the search, she could only come up with so many possibilities.

Then it occurred to her. Jane had the idea to reach out to the larger community and seek out those opportunities that existed beyond her immediate circle. So, Jane followed her intuition and began exploring two different avenues.

The first was to identify influencers and potential mentors who could connect her with bigger opportunities. This took her several months to accomplish, but she eventually found several willing and experienced mentors who could point her in the right direction.

The second avenue required a bit more legwork. Jane volunteered her time at a local nonprofit organization in order to gain first-hand experience in the field. She quickly found that while the pay may have been nominal, the connections she made and the experience she gained from such organizations was worth every penny.

Through these efforts, Jane broadened her outlook, connected with amazing professionals, and became better prepared for the future of her career. What she once thought was an uphill battle gradually shifted into a manageable task. Her decision to seek out growth opportunities ended up being a fruitful and rewarding one.

Chapter 23:
More Tips for Overcoming Negative Thinking

1. Learn to Notice Automatic Negative Thoughts

Most of the time, our thoughts happen automatically and go unnoticed. The first step in overcoming negative thinking is to become aware of what we're thinking. As soon as you notice the negative thought, make a conscious effort to stop and identify it.

2. Challenge Your Negative Thoughts

Don't accept your negative thoughts as facts. Once you are aware of your negative thoughts, you can challenge them and replace them with more positive ones. Ask yourself if the thought is realistic or if there is an alternative point of view.

3. Evaluate the Evidence

Take a closer look at the evidence. Is the thought really true or are there other possible explanations? Question the accuracy of the thought so you can better assess the situation and make better decisions.

4. Stay Grounded

Don't get caught up in "what if" scenarios. Focus on the facts and what is happening in the present. Stay anchored to reality and don't let your mind run wild with thoughts that may not be based in reality.

5. Step Back and Take a Break

When you find yourself stuck in a pattern of negative thinking, take a step back. Detach yourself from the situation for a few moments and get some perspective. Sometimes simply walking away from the situation can help you to break the cycle of negative thinking.

6. Focus on the Positive Aspects

Whenever possible, try to focus on the positive aspects of the situation. Even when faced with difficult circumstances, there may be some positive aspects that you can focus on. Focusing on the positive can help you to shift your focus away from the negative thoughts and feel more hopeful.

7. Find Healthy Outlets

Make sure to take care of yourself and find healthy outlets to manage your stress and emotions. This can include things like doing some light exercise, finding time to relax, or engaging in activities that bring you joy.

Chapter 24:
Harnessing the Power of Positive Visualization

Harnessing the power of positive visualization can be a powerful tool to help you reach your goals. This technique works by allowing you to imagine yourself in the future and actively pursue your dream. By visualizing the life that you want, you are more likely to experience it in reality.

Visualization is a form of meditation, which is the practice of focusing your attention in the present moment. When you focus your mind on a desired future outcome, you are more likely to achieve it. Visualization can be used to set goals, create new pathways to success, and connect your mind to the power of your subconscious.

When practicing positive visualization, it is important to keep your goal in mind and focus on the desired outcome. It is also important to keep your mental and emotional state positive. Picture yourself living the life that you want and take the time to imagine it in detail. Focus on the feeling of accomplishment, joy, and success that achieving your goals would bring.

To get the most out of positive visualization, it is important to practice it regularly. To begin, try to spend five to ten minutes each day envisioning the outcome you desire and connecting with the feelings of success. As you become more familiar with the practice, try to spend longer periods of time visualizing your goals.

Positive visualization has been proven to increase motivation, decrease stress, and move people towards their goals. By harnessing the power of this tool and actively engaging in visualization, you can take yourself closer to the future that you desire.

Chapter 25:
Cultivating a Positive Mindset

Having a positive mindset is essential for creating a happier, more fulfilling life. It's about learning to appreciate the good in life and to focus on the positive rather than the negative. It's about believing in yourself and having faith that things will work out. It's about being grateful for what you have and being kind and compassionate to yourself and others.

But cultivating a positive mindset doesn't happen overnight – it takes consistent effort and practice. Here are some tips to help you develop a more positive outlook on life:

1. Use affirmations. Affirmations are positive statements that help you focus on the good in life. They can help you shift your thinking from negative to positive and provide motivation and inspiration to take action.

2. Practice gratitude. Practicing gratitude can help you appreciate the good things in life and be more mindful of your thoughts. Take the time each day to think of three things you're grateful for and it will help you become more positive.

3. Surround yourself with positive people. It's important to surround yourself with people who are positive and supportive. This will help you stay motivated and inspired and will create a more positive environment for you to grow.

4. Find joy in the present moment. The present moment is all we have, so it's important to find joy and contentment in the here and now. This will help you stay positive and be in tune with the beauty that life has to offer.

5. Overcome negative thinking. Negative thinking can be a barrier to a positive mindset. To overcome it, it's important to practice self-

awareness and become aware of your thought patterns. When you catch yourself thinking negatively, replace those thoughts with more positive ones.

6. Build resilience and positive coping skills. Building resilience and positive coping skills is essential for staying positive in challenging times. Think of ways you can build resilience such as exercise, meditation, and journaling.

7. Practice self-care. Self-care is essential for cultivating a positive mindset. Make sure to take care of yourself, even when times get tough. Don't be afraid to ask for help when needed.

8. Be kind and compassionate to yourself. It's important to be kind and compassionate to yourself, especially when things don't go as planned. Forgive yourself for mistakes and remember that progress is always possible.

Cultivating a positive mindset is essential for living a happy, fulfilling life. It requires effort and consistency, but it's worth it. By following the tips above, you can develop a more positive outlook on life and create lasting change.

Chapter 26:
How to Deal With Difficult People

One of the most challenging aspects of life is learning how to deal with difficult people while still maintaining a positive attitude and outlook. Fortunately, there are some strategies that can help.

First, it is incredibly important to remember that no matter what behavior someone is exhibiting, their behavior is not a reflection on you or your worth. Difficult people may be aggressive and disrespectful, but how you respond to them and how you deal with the situation says more about you than it does about them.

One strategy for dealing with difficult people is to remain calm and take a step back from the situation. Taking a step back allows you to think more clearly and assess the situation from a more objective perspective. It can also help to disengage from the conversation and instead focus on investing your energy in positive thoughts and activities.

Next, it is important to remember that difficult people can often be quite good at manipulating or push people's buttons. When dealing with difficult people, try to avoid taking the bait or trying to do battle with those who are acting in a difficult manner. Instead, keep your focus on the issue and not the person.

One of the most important strategies for dealing with difficult people is to maintain your boundaries. Clearly state your boundaries and expectations at the start of an interaction, and be willing to walk away from situations that are not meeting those expectations.

Finally, do your best to keep a positive attitude and attitude towards yourself. Remind yourself that hard times pass, and that it is possible to turn any situation into an opportunity for personal growth. Be kind and patient with yourself, and believe in yourself and your ability to handle even the most challenging of people.

Chapter 27:
Releasing Stress and Letting Go

It can be difficult to let go of the stress in your life. Many of us worry over our daily problems, constantly looking for a solution. But sometimes the best thing to do is to take a step back and let go of your stress. Here are some tips to help you do just that.

1. Deep breathing: The power of deep breathing should not be underestimated. It helps to reduce stress levels, relaxes your body and centers your thoughts. Just five minutes of deep breathing can make a huge difference and start the process of releasing stress.

2. Exercise: Exercise helps to release endorphins that make you feel better. Even if you don't have time for a full workout, try to take short walks during the day or practice some simple stretches.

3. Change your perspective: It's often easy to feel overwhelmed by our problems. However, it can help to take a step back and try to look at them from a different angle. Seeing a problem from a different perspective can also help to put it into perspective and make it seem less daunting.

4. Mindful meditation: Practicing mindfulness can help to focus your attention on the present moment, rather than worrying about the future or dwelling on the past. Meditation can also help to reduce stress and anxiety levels.

5. Talk it out: When we bottle up our worries, they can become overwhelming and lead to stress. Talking to a trusted friend or relative can help to get things out and help you to see them in a different light.

6. Write it down: If talking isn't helpful, writing things down can help to organize and clarify our thoughts. This also gives us a

chance to analyze our worries in a more objective way.

By taking these steps, we can slowly start to release our stress and let go of it. Although it takes practice and commitment, it's worth it in the end!

Chapter 28: Choosing to See the Best in Others

In an effort to have a positive mindset and uphold our highest standards for ourselves and others, we must practice seeing the best in everyone and everything. When we open ourselves to the abundance of the Universe, choosing to see the best in the world around us, we are constantly rewarded.

The benefits to this mindset are far-reaching. Choosing to see the best in others raises our emotional and mental vibes, which can translate into physical energy and wellbeing, increased happiness, and healthier relationships with those we encounter. Positively orienting our view of the world and its people can also help us set our intentions, practice compassion and empathy, and be more open to new experiences and possibilities.

When we choose to see the best in others, the rewards are two-fold throughout our personal journeys. We attract positive energy, opportunity, and even those who support our highest values and goals. Simultaneously, we feel uplifted and rewarded through our own inner strength, joy, and inspiration.

Ultimately, choosing to see the best in others can be a beautiful and transformative practice that helps us recognize our highest selves and offers us unlimited potential as we connect more deeply and authentically with the world around us.

Chapter 29:
Connecting with Nature

Connecting with nature is becoming increasingly important as our lives become more and more technology-oriented. The Naturalist Movement in the mid-1800s focused on the idea of reconnecting with nature, and since then, many studies have shown that connecting with nature carries with it many physical and mental benefits. Nature has the ability to lower stress and negative emotions, provide us with physical health benefits, help us to become more mindful, and even boost creativity.

The physical health benefits of connecting with nature are numerous. Nature has been shown to reduce inflammation in the body, help to regulate the body's natural healing processes, and even help to boost the immune system. It can also help lower blood pressure and stress levels, improve sleep quality, and reduce feelings of depression and anxiety. All of these factors can contribute to an overall sense of well being and make us feel better each day.

Connecting with nature can also help to improve our mental health in many ways. Spending time in nature has been shown to help boost our creativity and make us more mindful. It can also help to reduce negative emotions and stress, which can have a positive impact on our overall mental health. Additionally, connecting with nature can help us to reconnect with ourselves and the world around us, and allow us to appreciate the beauty of the natural world.

Finally, the act of connecting with nature can also help us to better appreciate the environment around us and to stay mindful of our impact on the planet. This helps us to be more conscious of our choices and how they affect the planet as a whole. Additionally, spending time in nature can help us to build a sense of connection to the environment, resulting in a greater appreciation for the natural world and our ability to live in it.

In summary, connecting with nature can bring us physical and mental health benefits, as well as a greater appreciation for our environment. Taking the time to connect with nature and cherish its beauty is an important investment in our overall health and should be taken advantage of when we can.

Chapter 30:
Healthy Self-Talk and Self-Expression

Self-talk is the process by which you talk to yourself. It is a behavior that affects how you perceive yourself and the world around you. When you practice healthy self-talk, you can shape your thoughts, feelings, and behaviors in positive ways, leading to improved self-confidence and overall well-being.

When it comes to self-expression, it's all about learning to express your authentic self. Expressing yourself and your thoughts and feelings openly is essential for fostering healthy mental, emotional, and social relationships.

Start by being aware of your thoughts and feelings. Acknowledge and accept them as part of who you are. This can help you to develop a sense of self-acceptance, which will open the door to true self-expression and self-confidence.

Next, find a way to express your true self. This might be through writing, art, music, or dance, or any other form of creative expression. You may also find it helpful to use constructive self-talk to reassure and empower yourself.

Developing healthy self-talk and self-expression takes practice. Make sure to find time each day to both express yourself and practice positive self-talk. Remind yourself that these are both important practices that you can use to build a more positive attitude and sense of self. And remember, no one is perfect, so don't be afraid to make mistakes.

If self-expression comes easily to you, or if you have difficulty with it, it's important to practice patience and self-compassion. This can help you to feel supported, encouraged, and fostered as you go through the process.

Sometimes it's helpful to talk to a friend or professional to help you through this process, so don't be afraid to seek help if you need it.

Healthy self-talk and self-expression can help you to become the best version of yourself and to lead a happy and fulfilled life. By honoring your thoughts, feelings, and decisions, you can open the door to a new and positive mindset.

Chapter 31:
Clearing Away Mental Clutter

Though there are many causes of mental clutter, the key to having a clutter-free mind lies in clearing away our mental clutter and creating a sense of simplicity.

The easiest way to do this is to take some time out each day to relax and develop a solid calming routine. This could be something as simple as going outside for a walk, meditating, exercising, or catching up on a good book. Anything that can help you clear your head and provide a sense of peace and clarity is beneficial.

Another element of decluttering is to consciously focus on the present moment, instead of worrying about the past or stressing over the future. We cannot be in two mental places at once, so by focusing on the "here and now" and not rehashing the past or worrying the future, we can make room in our heads for more positive and productive thoughts.

Similarly, it is also important to practice acceptance and letting go. We cannot control everything, but what we can control is our reaction to the things that life throws at us. By practicing acceptance for the events and circumstances outside of our control and letting go of what we can't change, we can clear out space for gratitude and optimism.

Finally, when it comes to mental clutter, maintaining a healthy perspective is essential. Instead of getting wrapped up in the details of negative or stressful thoughts, try to look at the bigger picture and try to see the blessings that may be in store. By not focusing on the negative thoughts but looking for the silver lining in even the gloomiest of situations, we can start to sweep away our mental clutter.

Chapter 32:
Surrounding Yourself with Positive People

Surrounding yourself with positive people can be a great way to achieve your goals and stay motivated. Having a support system of positive and encouraging people in your life can be a huge boost and make it easier to get through difficult times.

First and foremost, if you're looking to improve your life, you should start focusing on cultivating and maintaining positive relationships with people. Take the time to talk to your friends, family members, and even co-workers about how you're feeling, about your goals, and about the progress you're making. Don't be afraid to be vulnerable; it's an important part of forming a deep bond.

One way to ensure that you're surrounding yourself with positivity is to join groups and organizations that share your interests and goals. Look for local groups devoted to topics like exercise, dieting, or healthy living. Even joining an online group that's devoted to a particular passion can be helpful.

It's also important to watch what you share on social media. Before you post, ask yourself, "Does this post promote positive feelings and thoughts?" Strive to create an online presence that focuses on positivity, or even select a few close friends and family that you only share your positive updates with.

Finally, sometimes, you may find yourself in a negative atmosphere. At times, it's best to remove yourself from negative conversations and groups. If you're feeling overwhelmed in a particular situation, be sure to take time out for yourself, even if it's just a few moments.

By surrounding yourself with positive people, it's easier to stay motivated and remain on track to reach your goals. It's important to make sure that those around you are supportive and encouraging, not critical or judgmental. If you're looking to make positive changes in your life, this is the best way to go about it.

Chapter 33:
Reframing the Way You Approach Challenges

As you journey through life, you're going to encounter more and more challenging situations. It's not enough to just assume that these challenges will never end – you need to look for ways to reframe and approach them in a positive manner in order to develop the skills and fortitude to persevere.

The first step in reframing is to recognize that challenges are not something to be avoided, but rather something to be used as a catalyst to achieve greatness. When you approach a situation or challenge with the mindset of using it as an opportunity to better yourself, you can create a platform which allows you to become successful.

Another key component in reframing your approach is to see the challenge as a learning experience. While it may seem to you that the problem is insurmountable, with a bit of patience and persistence you can use the experience as a learning tool. As you confront and address any roadblock that you face, you will gain valuable insights and develop your capability to face future challenges that come your way.

Finally, one of the most effective strategies for reframing the way you approach challenges is to take a step back and look for the positive elements of a situation. By doing so, you will gain a greater perspective of any situation, and this will help you to take a more proactive approach. Concentrate on the positive outcomes of the challenge, and you will be able to focus your energy on what needs to happen in order to get to the end result that you desire.

By reframing the way you view and tackle challenging situations, you will be able to develop an improved attitude and mindset that will help you stay on course and achieve success, no matter how difficult the situation.

Chapter 34:
When Stress is Unavoidable

Stress is an unavoidable part of life. Everyone experiences it to various degrees, and it's important to have coping strategies in place to help deal with it when it arises. The first step to combatting stress is to identify the source of it. Once you know where the stress is coming from, you can more easily decide how to address it.

There are many different ways to cope with stress. One of the most important is to be mindful. Taking a few moments each day to pause and check in with yourself, your thoughts, and how you're feeling can be a helpful way to process and release any tension. Additionally, exercise is a great coping mechanism for stress. Moving your body in some way can be a great way to release any built-up anticipation or pent-up energy.

Staying positive is also imperative when dealing with stress. While it can be difficult to remain optimistic, shifting your perspective can go a long way. Instead of only letting your worries and fears take over, look for the positive in your situation and focus on that. Not only will it help redirect your thoughts, but it can also give you newfound perspective and hope.

Finally, it can be helpful to talk to someone. Connecting with a friend or loved one can give you the reassurance you need to help manage your stress. Likewise, many people find talking to a professional to be beneficial. Whether it's a therapist, counselor, or life coach, enlisting the help of someone who can listen and guide you can be extremely impactful.

At the end of the day, it's important to remember that stressing over something won't make it go away, so try to keep a level head. When stress is unavoidable, use these coping skills to stay positive and process your feelings in healthy ways.

1. Take a few deep breaths and focus on slowing down your heart rate.

2. Exercise or go for a walk to release physical and mental tension.

3. Identify your triggers and think through potential solutions.

4. Talk to a friend or family member.

5. Practice mindful activities like yoga or meditation.

6. Create a plan to manage the situation.

7. Practice healthy coping mechanisms like journaling or listening to music.

8. Get enough sleep, nutrition, and hydration.

9. Take a break and focus on self-care activities.

10. Seek professional help and resources for extra support.

Chapter 35:
The Benefits of Journaling for Positive Thinking

Journaling can be a powerful tool in improving positive thinking and personal growth. Studies have shown that people who journal on a regular basis have improved self-esteem and increased motivation. By taking the time to reflect on our thoughts and feelings, we can gain insight into our own behavior, enabling us to make healthier choices and boost our overall mental health.

Many people think that journaling is only for writers and creative types, but the truth is that everyone can benefit from taking the time to jot down their musings. Keeping a journal allows us to express ourselves in a safe, private space. As we look back through our entries, patterns may emerge that can provide valuable insight into difficult issues we are facing.

Journaling can also help us recognize negative thinking patterns, such as rumination and catastrophizing. When faced with challenging situations, we can recognize that it is not the end of the world, even if it feels that way in the moment. This can help us develop a more rational and realistic view of the situation, which in turn can bolster our confidence and raise our mood.

Finally, journaling can help us appreciate the positive events in our life more deeply. By writing down the moments of joy, gratitude, and connection we experience, we can look back and recognize the moments of beauty that we may otherwise overlook. This can help us to even out our emotional highs and lows and create a greater sense of meaning and purpose in our lives.

Journaling is an incredibly powerful tool, and the benefits of its practice can be seen in all aspects of life. Taking the time to reflect on our thoughts and feelings can have a profound effect on our self-confidence and mental health, allowing us to create positive thinking patterns and enhance personal growth.

Chapter 36:
Gratitude Journal

A gratitude journal is a journal in which you record moments or items in your life that you are thankful for. In the journal, you can reflect on the positive things that have happened to you, or the moments that lifted your spirits, or even the people or things that have made a positive impact on your life. Gratitude journals can also be used to record life experiences or events that have made you appreciate life's beauty and complexity, celebrate joy, and help you gain perspective.

Gratitude journals can help you focus on what is good in life, rather than on the negative aspects. Practicing gratitude can be a great way to consciously reassess the abundance and joy available to you, and it can also have a very positive effect on your emotional state. Gratitude journalling can help reduce anxiety and depression, increase resilience, and enhance satisfaction with life.

Creating a gratitude journal can be done in different ways. Some people choose to write down a few words that express what they are thankful for each day. Others use pictures, videos, quotes, music, or artwork. You could create a "Happiness Jar" by writing down events or experiences on pieces of paper, and then shaking the jar to show physical representation of your combination of positive thoughts and experiences. There is no wrong way to express the gratitude that you feel— you just need to make sure that you're engaging in meaningful reflection and sharing the things that bring you joy.

Chapter 37:
The Benefits of a Gratitude Journal

Gratitude journals have become increasingly popular in recent years, and for a good reason. The benefits of a gratitude journal are far-reaching. Keeping one can help you foster a sense of appreciation, reduce stress levels, focus on the present moment, and even boost your overall wellbeing.

Expressing gratitude promotes an encouraging attitude, leading to an overall more positive outlook on the world around you. Whereas a regular journal focuses on documenting and analyzing the events of your day, a gratitude journal instead helps you reflect and find an appreciation for the circumstances, people, and things in your life.

In addition to providing mental and emotional boosts, keeping a gratitude journal even offers a physiological advantage. Studies have connected writing about positive experiences to improved mood, as well as physical health benefits such as greater resistance to illnesses and faster healing times.

Focusing on the here and now is a key element of practicing gratitude. It can be easy to slip into a state of anxiety, regret, or worry over the choices of the past or the plans of the future. When you make a practice of taking a few minutes each day to record what you're grateful for, it helps center your thoughts and reconnect you with the present moment.

Most importantly, taking time to recognize and give thanks for what you have can entirely transform the relationships and moments you share, as well as create a foundation of appreciation and kindness that will follow you through life. A gratitude journal is a powerful tool to cultivate those attitudes, build positive habits, and reap the rewards of a grateful outlook.

Chapter 38:
Gratitude Journaling: Step-by-Step

Creating a gratitude journal can be a great way to reflect on your day and remind yourself of all you have to be grateful for. Here is how to start a gratitude journal:

1. Choose a notebook or journal that you like. Making it pretty and enjoyable to look at encourages you to write in it regularly.

2. Make a few specific rules or guidelines for journaling. For example, you might decide to write 3-5 things each day that you're

grateful for, or just write as much as you'd like about any gratitude topic.

3. Pick a time every day you can dedicate to writing in your gratitude journal. You could do it first thing in the morning, before going to bed at night, or even on your lunch break.

4. When it's time to write, start by focusing on the present moment. Notice the sights and sounds around you, take a few deep breaths, and allow yourself to be mindful of your environment.

5. Begin writing down your thoughts of gratitude. It can be anything from how your best friend is there for you to how much you appreciate the sunrise every morning. Let your words flow and don't worry if some days you don't have much to write — it's all part of the process!

6. Keep your gratitude journal with you wherever you go, so you can take a few moments throughout the day to reflect on your blessings.

Creating a gratitude journal can be an easy, yet powerful practice that can help you stay focused on all you have to be thankful for.

With these few simple steps, you're on your way to creating a space for yourself where you can appreciate and be grateful for all the positive moments in your life.

Chapter 39:
The Happiness Jar

A happiness jar is a simple, meaningful, and powerful tool that can help bring more joy to your life. It consists of writing down your moments of happiness, gratitude, and accomplishments on small pieces of paper and then placing them in a jar. It's a physical representation of all the beautiful and positive moments you've experienced in life and serves as an outlet to keep track of these positive moments.

The idea of the happiness jar is to remind us of the good in our lives and to focus on the positives, no matter what is happening in our day. Everyone experiences highs and lows, but a happiness jar allows us to remember that even on a bad day we have a lot to be thankful for. These happy moments can be anything from finding a quarter on the ground to getting a promotion at work.

Using a happiness jar is easy and requires minimal effort. When you experience a moment of joy, write it down on a piece of paper and place it in the jar. It doesn't take much time, and the more moments you capture, the fuller your jar will become. When the jar is full, you can take it out and read through your notes and recall all the blessings in your life.

This simple practice can help you remember the reasons that you are happy, feel gratitude for what you have, and encourage positive thinking. The happiness jar is a powerful tool to have in your life, and it's an easy way to stay connected to all the beautiful moments you've experienced.

Chapter 40:
Vision Boards

A vision board is a visual tool designed to help you visualize and manifest the things you want to achieve in life. It serves as a reminder of your goals and aspirations, allowing you to bring them to life.

Vision boards can help you focus on the positive, create achievable goals, and ultimately, help you become a better version of yourself. They can be filled with inspiring images, quotes or words, and symbols that are meaningful to you and help keep you motivated on the path to success.

Creating a vision board can be a powerful exercise that helps you clarify your life values, set realistic objectives, and focus on what matters most to you. By using a vision board, you can have something tangible to refer to daily that will keep you motivated and remind you of what you are working towards.

You can create your vision board with anything that is meaningful to you, such as photographs, words, and symbols. It can also be filled with inspiring quotes and messages that remind you of your purpose, create motivation, and help you stay focused on achieving your goals.

If you are interested in creating a vision board, start by gathering materials, such as magazines, newspapers, photographs, and markers. Once you have your materials, pick a spot where your vision board can hang and be a constant reminder of your goals.

Begin assembling your vision board by cutting out images and phrases that resonate with you. As you put your vision board together, try to focus on the feeling that each element evokes. You want your vision board to inspire and motivate you towards your goals, so it should motivate you to work hard, set long-term goals, and strive to live a life of purpose and joy.

Once you have created your vision board, hang it in a place where you can easily see it every day. Take steps to make sure your action items are achievable and use the vision board as a reminder of the life that you want to create.

Vision boards can serve as a powerful tool to help you achieve the life of your dreams. With focus, dedication, and a clear vision of your future, anything is possible.

Chapter 41:
Mantra Cards

Mantra Cards are cards that contain a powerful and positive message to help an individual live a more balanced and fulfilled life. Each card contains an inspirational phrase or saying designed to motivate, inspire, and bring forth a positive attitude and outlook. Mantra Cards can help people keep a positive attitude by providing a reminder of the positive aspects of their life, and the possibilities that lie ahead.

The mantras on Mantra Cards are often based on Eastern spiritual traditions, including Buddhism, Christianity, Hinduism, and other ancient wisdom. Each card contains a unique mantra which can be used to strengthen one's spirit and bring clarity and inner insight.

Mantra Cards are often used as a form of self-care and personal growth, as well as to help with stress relief and relaxation. Each card has its own purpose and can be chosen depending on the individual's needs. Commonly used mantras include phrases such as, "I will always choose love", "Everything is as it should be", and "I am enough".

Mantra Cards are great tools to help an individual stay motivated, inspired, and focused on what matters most to them. Not only do they offer a daily reminder of positivity, but they also provide a source of comfort and support. By using Mantra Cards regularly, individuals can build their inner strength and resilience, and ultimately live a more fulfilling life.

Chapter 42:
Why do I Automatically Jump to Negative Thoughts

Our emotional responses can be triggered by any number of factors, and sometimes, even the most innocuous of comments or situations can lead to a sudden barrage of negative thinking. This is because our emotional reactions are often determined by established neural pathways in our brain.

These pathways are responsible for making decisions quickly and efficiently based on our past experiences. In other words, it is the neural infrastructure that helps us to immediately recognize familiar patterns, and to react accordingly.

When it comes to our emotional responses, the same is true. We all have certain neural pathways that have been established over time, and which govern the way we think, behave, and respond. And if any of these pathways contain negative associations, we are likely to react to a situation with a negative response, without blinking an eye.

For example, if we have had a negative experience in the past that triggered negative thinking or feeling - such as being bullied, or going through a difficult break-up - our brain may recognize a similar situation and automatically jump to the same negative conclusion.

As such, if we are presented with a similar situation, our brain may react in the same way. Our thoughts may be clouded with feelings of inadequacy or self-doubt, leaving us unable to think straight and allowing us to become overwhelmed by negative thoughts.

These pathways may be difficult to recognize and difficult to change, but identifying the negative pathways and taking steps to change them can help to prevent us from automatically jumping to negative thoughts.

Chapter 43:
Neural Plasticity

The brain is an incredibly complex organ, composed of billions of neurons that are constantly firing off signals as we go about our daily lives. In order to understand how continuing to practice positive thinking can grow new neural pathways in the brain, it is important to first understand what a neural pathway is, and how it works. Essentially, a neural pathway is a network of neurons that are connected by synapses and are responsible for carrying information from one part of the brain to another. When a person experiences something or has a thought, the neurons associated with that experience or thought will fire off a signal and create a pathway. This is what is known as neural plasticity, which refers to the brain's ability to create new pathways based on experience and continue to form new pathways and change existing ones.

Chapter 44:
The Effects of Positive Thinking in the Brain

We have known for some time now that positive thinking has beneficial effects on the brain. Studies have found that thinking positively has been linked to increased cognitive functioning and an improved mood. Additionally, it has been suggested that positive thinking can increase the level of "neurogenesis", a process by which new neurons are created. This process can be likened to creating new pathways in the brain, and has been linked to improved memory and learning. While this is only speculation, it does suggest that positive thinking can have a direct effect on the physical structure of the brain.

Positive thinking has been shown to have a wide range of positive effects on the brain. Studies have shown that positive thinking can boost brain power, reduce stress hormones, and even increase activity in the parts of the brain associated with emotional regulation and decision-making.

The power of positive thinking has been studied in various contexts, including the workplace and medicine. In the workplace, research has found that when individuals are in a positive state of mind, they are better able to think clearly, take action and make decisions. They are also more resilient to stress and can better manage difficult tasks.

Studies on the effects of positive thinking on the brain have been conducted in a variety of scenarios, including in cancer patients. In these studies, researchers found that cancer patients who had higher levels of positive thinking experienced reduced stress and experienced better overall quality of life.

In addition to reducing stress and increasing quality of life, positive thinking has been shown to have long-term effects on the brain's health. Studies have found that individuals who practice positive thinking are less likely to develop Alzheimer's disease and other forms of dementia. The mechanism of how positive thinking affects brain health is still unclear, but researchers believe that the act of positive thinking may stimulate the production of certain neural transmitters, which can improve memory and learning.

Furthermore, positive thinking can also enhance creativity. People who adopt a positive mindset are more likely to think outside the box and effectively solve problems while developing novel ideas.

Overall, the effects of positive thinking on the brain are clear. Positive thinking can reduce stress, improve cognitive function, increase creativity, and even promote better brain health in the long term. Therefore, it is important to cultivate a positive outlook in order to benefit from the full potential of the mind.

Chapter 45:
Creating New Pathways with Positive Thinking

There is now a body of research that suggests that continuing to practice positive thinking can lead to the creation of new neural pathways in the brain. Positive thinking has been found to increase emotional regulation and resilience, which can lead to increased levels of overall well-being. As neural pathways become more established, knowledge, skills, and emotional agility are improved and maintained. Additionally, research has shown that the hippocampus, an area of the brain that is related to our ability to learn and remember, is more active when an individual engages in positive thinking.

Ultimately, continuing to practice positive thinking can have a profound effect on the brain and its ability to create new pathways. Not only is this a great way to promote overall health and wellbeing, but it can also lead to improved cognitive functioning and emotional regulation. With regular practice, neural pathways are established and reinforced, leading to better functioning and an improved lifestyle.

Chapter 46:
Defaulting to Positive Thinking

We discussed earlier that neural pathways refer to the connections between two areas of the brain. When a person learns a new behavior or thought pattern, a neural pathway is formed, allowing a person to easily access these behaviors or thoughts in the future. As such, forming new neural pathways can be extremely helpful for those looking to default to positive thinking.

The first step in creating new neural pathways for positive thinking is awareness and mindfulness. By becoming aware of your thoughts and feelings as they occur, you can identify negative thinking and replace it with positive thinking. As you practice this positive replacement process regularly, your brain will learn that this is preferable to defaulting to negative thinking.

The next step is to practice positive thinking regularly. Whether it's through self-talk or identifying happy moments and events, commit to replacing more and more of your negative thoughts with positive ones. Visualization techniques can also be useful in this regard, allowing you to envision yourself confidently overcoming personal or professional obstacles.

The last step is to get specific. If there are certain situations that frequently bring on negative thinking, make sure to focus on them and what positive thoughts or behaviors you can use to combat them. This practice can also be used to proactively prepare for future situations, so you're prepared to immediately default to positive thinking in the future.

By practicing these steps, you will begin to form new neural pathways dedicated to positive thinking. Eventually, with practice and dedication, you will be able to default to positive thinking more automatically and consistently.

Chapter 47:
Positive Thinking and Alzheimer's

Alzheimer's disease is a progressive neurological disorder that affects millions of people around the world. It is a degenerative disorder that slowly destroys the brain and leads to memory loss, confusion, and ultimately death. Although there is no known cure for Alzheimer's, there are ways to prevent and battle the disease through positive thinking. In this chapter, we will be exploring the power of positive thinking and how it can be used to prevent and battle Alzheimer's.

Positive thinking has been shown to have a number of health benefits, including reducing stress and improving overall mental health. It has also been linked to improved physical health, including a decrease in the risk of developing Alzheimer's disease. Positive thinking can help to reduce the risk of developing Alzheimer's by reducing stress levels and improving overall mental health. Additionally, positive thinking can help to improve cognitive functioning, which is important for preventing and battling Alzheimer's.

Positive thinking can also help to improve the quality of life for those already living with Alzheimer's. It can help to reduce stress and anxiety, which can help to improve overall mental health. Additionally, positive thinking can help to reduce the symptoms of Alzheimer's, such as memory loss and confusion. Finally, positive thinking can help to improve the mood and outlook of those affected by Alzheimer's, which can help to reduce the feelings of isolation and depression that are often associated with the disease.

In conclusion, positive thinking can be an effective tool in preventing and battling Alzheimer's. It can help to reduce stress and improve overall mental health, which can help to reduce the risk of developing Alzheimer's.

Additionally, it can help to improve the quality of life for those already living with Alzheimer's. Finally, positive thinking can help to reduce the symptoms of Alzheimer's and improve the mood and outlook of those affected by the disease. For these reasons, positive thinking is an important tool in the fight against Alzheimer's.

Chapter 48:
Positive Thought Brainwaves and Physical Reality

Brainwaves are electrical signals that the brain produces in response to various stimuli. These signals are measured in hertz (Hz) and can range from very low frequencies (delta waves) to very high frequencies (gamma waves). It has long been thought that these brainwaves can have an effect on physical reality, but until recently, this has been largely unexplored. In this chapter, we will be exploring the potential of brainwaves and how they can affect physical reality.

Brainwaves have been shown to have a variety of effects on physical reality. For example, low-frequency delta waves have been linked to increased relaxation, improved sleep, and improved immunity. On the other hand, high-frequency gamma waves have been linked to increased alertness, improved memory, and enhanced creativity. Additionally, certain brainwave frequencies have been linked to improved physical performance, such as increased strength, speed, and endurance.

The human brain is a complex and powerful organ, capable of producing a wide variety of electrical signals. These signals, known as brainwaves, are responsible for the many processes that take place in the brain, from thought and memory to emotion and behavior.

But what if these brainwaves could be harnessed to affect physical reality? What if these electrical signals could be used to manifest our thoughts into reality? The concept of using brainwaves to manifest our reality is not a new one, and has been around for some time. It is possible to alter physical reality with brainwaves, and this chapter will explore the various ways in which this can be done.

First, we'll look at the concept of neuroplasticity, which is the ability of the brain to rewire itself and form new neuronal connections. This process is driven by the electrical signals produced by the brain. Neuroplasticity can be used to create new pathways in the brain, which can then be used to manifest our thoughts into reality.

Next, we'll look at the concept of neurofeedback, which is the process of using electrical signals from the brain as feedback loops to control physical processes. Neurofeedback can be used to alter physical reality by making changes to the brainwaves, which can then be used to manifest our thoughts into reality.

Finally, we'll look at the concept of self-hypnosis, which is the process of using our own thoughts and beliefs to alter our reality. Self-hypnosis can be used to manifest our thoughts into reality by altering the brainwaves and allowing us to access our subconscious mind.

Brainwaves may also have an effect on the physical environment. For example, certain frequencies have been shown to influence temperature, humidity, and air pressure. Additionally, they may have an effect on plant growth, animal behavior, and even the weather. Finally, brainwaves may be able to influence the behavior of other people, as certain frequencies have been linked to increased empathy and improved communication.

Research has shown that positive brain waves can be contagious and can have a positive effect on others. It is believed that when someone has a positive thought, their brain waves are picked up by the brain of someone nearby, and this can trigger a positive thought in the other person. This is known as the "mirror neuron effect," and it can be used to spread positive energy and help create a more positive atmosphere in any environment. By focusing on positive thoughts and sending out positive brain waves, we can help create more positive energy in our lives and the lives of those around us.

It is also believed that positive thought brain waves can attract the physical environment around you, drawing towards you the things you think about. This phenomenon is known as the Law of Attraction, and it is based on the idea that like attracts like. By focusing on positive thoughts and sending out positive brain waves, we can attract positive energy and experiences into our lives. This can help us manifest our goals and dreams, as well as create a more positive environment around us. By focusing on positive thoughts and sending out positive brain waves, we can attract positive energy and experiences into our lives.

By understanding how the brainwaves associated with positive thinking can be used to alter physical reality, we can gain more control over our own lives and manifest our thoughts into reality. For these reasons, it is important to understand the potential of positive thinking and how it can be used to our advantage. With practice and dedication we are able to unlock the full potential of the brainwaves associated with positive thinking and use them to improve our physical and mental wellbeing.

Chapter 49:
Sustaining Positive Thinking Over Time

In order to sustain positive thinking over time, it is important to focus on self-care and positive habits.

Self-care is essential for sustaining positive thinking. It is important to set aside time each day to focus on yourself and your well-being. Taking time for yourself can include activities such as exercise, relaxation, mediation, and spending time with loved ones. Self-care can be a great way to clear your head and focus on positive thoughts.

In addition to self-care, positive habits are a key to sustaining positive thinking. This can be something as simple as setting aside time each day to think positively. A great way to do this is to write down three things that you're grateful for. Doing this daily helps to keep you in a positive mindset and allows you to focus on the good in your life.

Another important step to sustaining positive thinking is to surround yourself with positive people. Positive thinking is contagious and spending time with people who bring out the best in you will make it easier to maintain a positive mindset.

Finally, it's important to stay away from negative influences as much as possible. There will always be people who try to bring you down with their negative opinions and outlook. It's important to recognize these people and to remain focused on the positive.

By following these steps, you can ensure that you'll be able to sustain positive thinking over time. Think positively, take care of yourself, keep good company, and stay away from negative influences. With these steps, you will be able to maintain a positive mindset and sustain positive thinking in the long run.